Antonio
VIVALDI

Magnificat
RV 610/611

Edited by
Clayton Westermann

Vocal Score
Klavierauszug

SERENISSIMA MUSIC, INC.

CONTENTS

1. Magnificat (Chorus) 1

2. Et Exultavit (Soprano, Alto, and Tenor Soli and Chorus) 3

2a. Et Exultavit (Alternate version – for Apollonia) 10

2b. Quia Respexit (Alternate version – for La Bolognese) 15

2c. Quia Fecit (Alternate version – for Chiaretta) 20

3. Et Misericordia (Chorus) 24

4. Fecit Potentiam (Chorus) 33

5. Deposuit (Chorus) 37

6. Esurientes (Duet for Two Sopranos) 41

6a. Esurientes (Alternate version – for Ambrosina) 46

7. Suscepit Israel (Chorus) 50

8. Sicut Locutus (Trio for Soprano, Alto, and Bass) 52

8a. Sicut Locutus (Alternate version – for Albetta) 59

9. Gloria (Chorus) 64

ORCHESTRA

2 Oboes (No.8), Bassoon (opt.), Keyboard,
Violin I, Violin II, Viola, Violoncello, Double Bass

MAGNIFICAT
RV 610/611

1. Magnificat Anima Mea

Antonio Vivaldi
Edited by Clayton Westermann

SERENISSIMA MUSIC, INC.

2. Et Exultavit

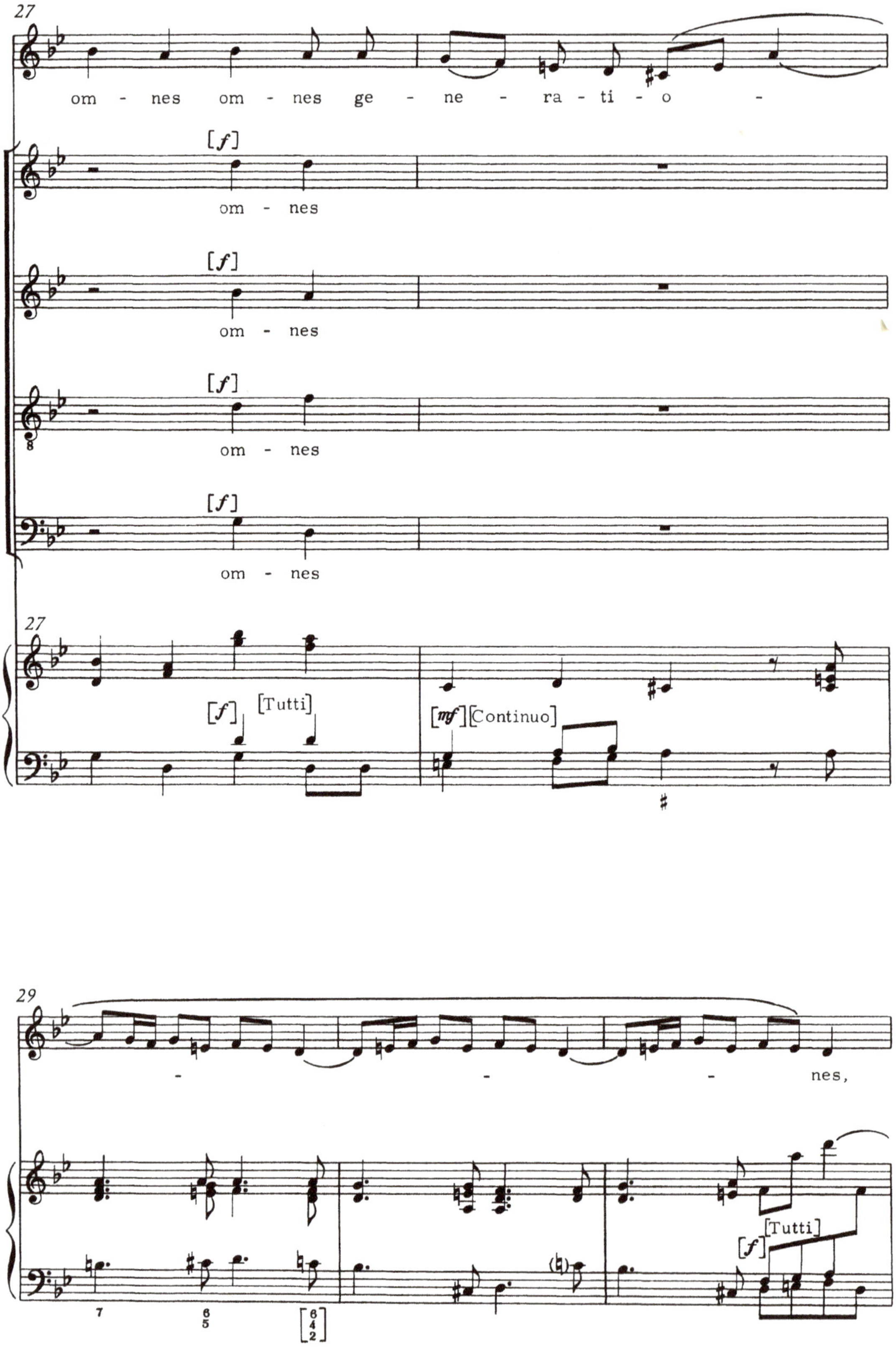
27
om - nes om - nes ge - ne - ra - ti - o -
[f]
om - nes
[f]
om - nes
[f]
om - nes
[f]
om - nes
27
[f] [Tutti]
[mf] [Continuo]
29
- - - nes,
[Tutti]
[f]

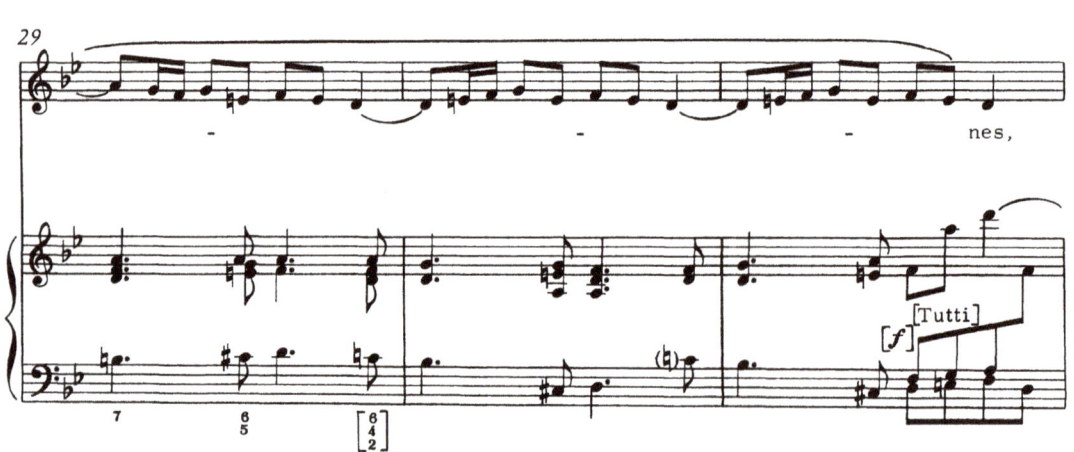

2a. Et Exultavit
(Alternate version – for Apollonia)

* Cadenza

2b. Quia Respexit
(Alternate version - for La Bolognese)

2c. Quia Fecit
(Alternate version - for Chiaretta)

* [Cadenza]

3. Et Misericordia

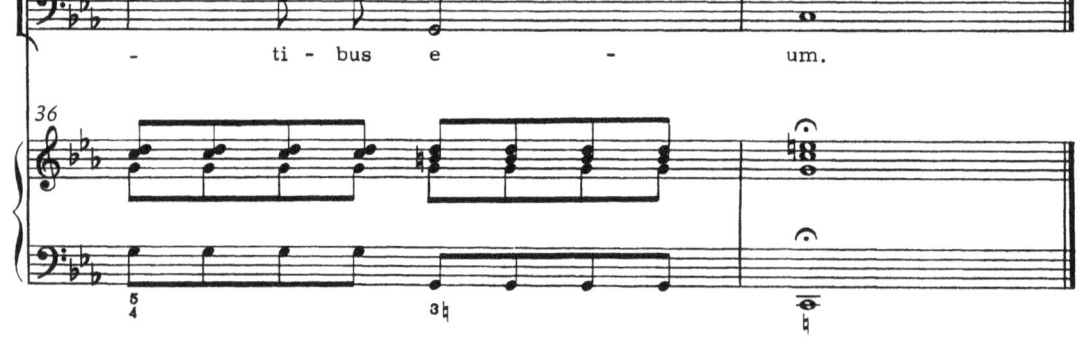

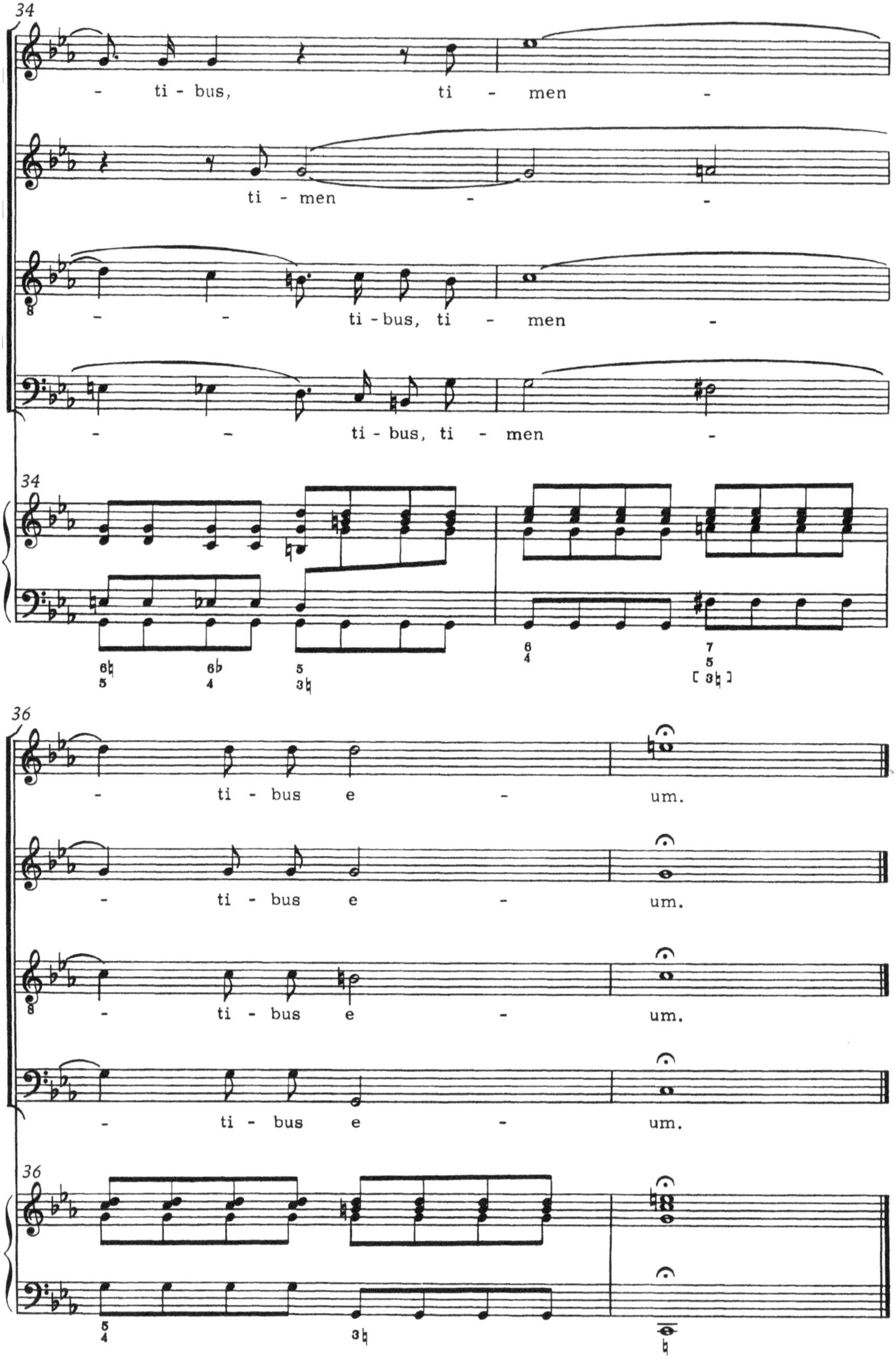
34
- ti - bus, ti - men -
ti - men - -
- - ti - bus, ti - men -
- - ti - bus, ti - men -
34
36
- ti - bus e - um.
- ti - bus e - um.
- ti - bus e - um.
- ti - bus e - um.
36

4. Fecit Potentiam

5. Deposuit

6. Esurientes

6a. Esurientes
(Alternate version - for Ambrosina)

* repeat the vowel sound on this note

* repeat the vowel sound on this note

* repeat the vowel sound on this note

7. Suscepit Israel

8. Sicut Locutus

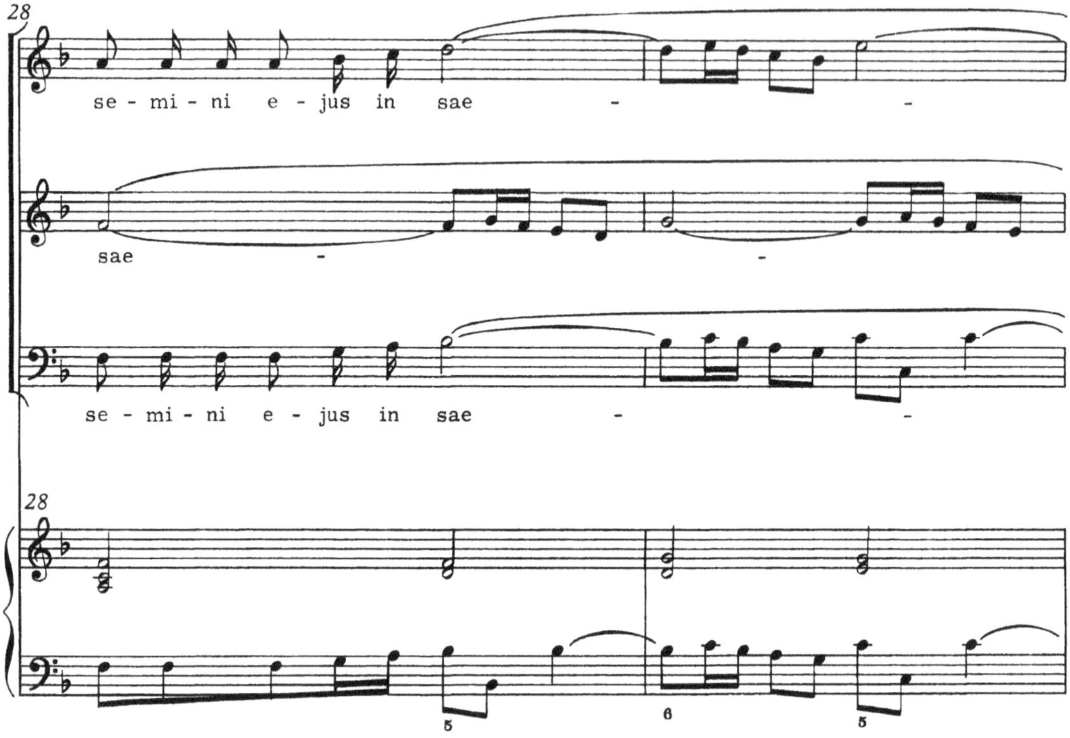
28
se - mi - ni e - jus in sae - -
sae - -
se - mi - ni e - jus in sae - -
28
5 6 5

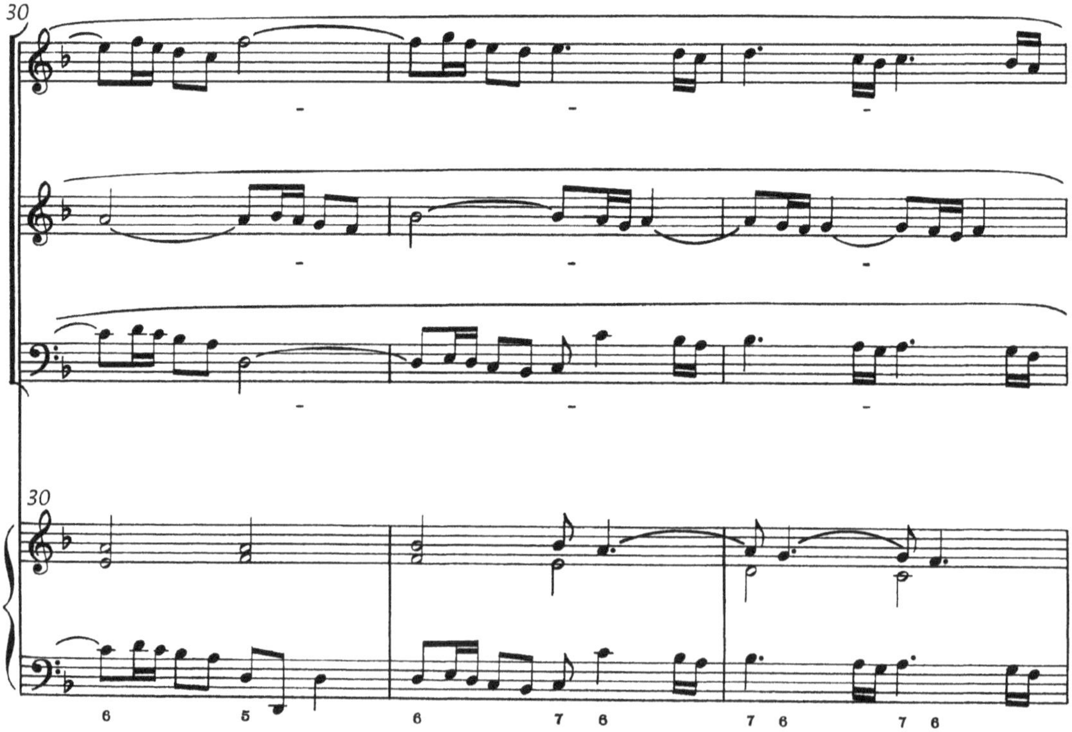
30
- - -
- - -
- - -
30
6 5 6 7 6 7 6 7 6

8a. Sicut Locutus
(Alternate version - for Albetta)

9. Gloria

www.ingramcontent.com/pod-product-compliance
Lightning Source LLC
Chambersburg PA
CBHW081348040426
42450CB00015B/3356